When You Love Someone

A Collection of Poetry

Marcel Cole

When You Love Someone: A Collection of Poetry

Copyright © 2020 by Marcel Cole

Published by Semaj Publishing

ISBN: 978-0-9981103-6-3

Printed in the United States of America. All rights reserved under the International Copyright Law.

Contents and/or cover may not reproduced in whole or in part in any form without the express written consent of the Publisher.

Contents

Dedication

The Enlightenment to My Soul 7
Can I Be 8
God's Cure 10
God's Scenery...11
Grow Old with Me..................................13
I Want To Get To Know You 15
I Wish 17
Life's Atonement....................................19
If I Had My Way.....................................23
If You Only Knew...................................24
In My Life 26
Independence Day 27
Love is Pain 29
Rainbow in the Sky 30
A Rainbow in the Sky 32
So Many Reasons 34
The Existence of a Matchless Beauty 36
This One Thing I Do Know 38
Those Eight Weeks 39

What Must I Do 41
What Would It Take 42
When a Man Loves a Woman 45
When Will My Time Come 47

This is a dedication to a woman who has the duplicity of being beautiful mentally and physically. This woman has touched my life in a way that I have become a better man in the process. I want her to know that her being a part of my life has made a great and a positive influence and I hate to admit but I am still in love with her, Samantha Abiola Israel.

The Enlightenment to My Soul

This is enlightenment to my soul that lifted the burden of trying to please you.

So every time you came my way, I realized that it was not meant for us to,

Be together and to know you better than I do.

So to know you where you are and what you are doing, I don't care but what is true,

Is that I realized that I am better now and things are great without you.

If you were to come around, you would not be in focus where my eyes can see.

The life I am looking for is one of stability and the single life is where I like to be.

I am a lot happier and I, Marcel Cole, is on a roll.

You think you know but you have no idea, that this is "The Enlightenment to My Soul".

"Can I Be"

Words cannot express the way I feel for you.

If you let me into your heart, I will always be true.

I want to be your everything but I know that it takes time.

There isn't a mountain that is high enough that we cannot climb.

I am learning to be upfront with what I feel I need to say.

I want to know that between you and I, everything is ok.

You have this glow about you that can light up the world.

I hope that out of that shell I have found a pearl.

You are special to me and I love your smile.

I wish after your class, we could spend time together for a while.

I would like it if we could sit on a bench and talk about you and me.

I want to be more than a friend to you and that is not lie, can't you see.

I know you get your fair share of guys who just talk but that is all they are about.

I am showing you that I want to be there and I am not about filling your head with doubt.

I want to show you who I am and what I stand for.

In the future, I just want to be all you need and more.

I want to be in your life and I need you to see,

That I want to be your best friend, so are you willing to be an influence on what, "Can I Be"?

God's Cure

I know that doctors sometimes do not have a cure.

You told me to bring you green tea a half-past four.

It seems like I have been traveling the medicine hall of fame.

Traveling the globe to find a cure for a cold for you, I do not feel shame.

Taking flights back and forth and always first class.

I thank God so much for the buddy pass.

I know you are feeling down like you are under a spell.

I pray to God that you will be on your feet soon and feeling well.

God's Scenery

When I look out on the ocean, as the sun is about to set.

God's scenery is so beautiful and is something I will never forget.

There is another beauty out there that is so captivating at the very sight.

You're that beauty and I love you with all my might.

I want to experience the joy of looking into your eyes.

I want this relationship with you to be the truth and no lies.

I see God in you and I look and see no disguise.

You are precious to me and when I look at my reflection in the mirror.

Day by day, God shows me things and they are starting to be clearer.

I am attracted to you and your conversation is one of a kind.

While I am cooking dinner, we are conversing over a glass of wine.

The unsurpassed beauty can be seen through the eyes willing to embrace it,

Looking at God's scenery through your eyes is so exquisite.

Grow Old with Me

I always think of what it would be like to wake up next to you every morning.

I would be the happiest man on earth if my wish came true.

If you were to help me with my wish, I will forever love you.

I have been thinking over again and again of the joy of knowing;

That I am confident of how I feel about you and when I tell you, your face starts glowing.

There is that smile I love to see and that look in your eyes.

I want to experience life with you to the fullest and reach the prize.

What I mean by this is that I want us to grow together in love.

We have this connection that was given to us by the Almighty God above.

I love what we have and I can't see us going our separate ways.

If you give your hand, I won't leave you until the end of my days.

I want to forever be by your side and for you to know that I am here.

I want to be that understanding soul mate and let you know that I will always care.

I hope that one day in the future you will see,

That out of all my wishes to come true, I wish for you to grow old with me.

I Want To Get To Know You

I want to get to know you but I don't know where to start or what to say.

I feel that my eyes give me away what I feel but cannot say.

So this poem is my way of expressing how I feel and I hope it comes across in a way of respect.

If we were to be together, I would show you the attention you need and would never neglect

Your feelings toward me or abuse the love that you will give to me.

I would show you how a guy can be a true friend and not cross that line or boundary.

My feelings, I try to keep bottled up inside because of what I been through,

It's hard to digest the thought of a life without you.

You are very beautiful and I know of that you are well aware,

So I will let you know that sometimes I try not to stare,

I try hard to wake myself out of the trance I am in when I don't have a clue,

In my approach, I am stagnant with what to say or do,

With my hopes extremely high, I want to get to know you.

I Wish

Daffodils and lilies she loves mixed the scent of a daisy

Wanting to know her inner secrets
Some think I am sweet and some think I am crazy

I wish I was born in the shadow of her presence

I want to smell the scent of her perfume and her pure essence

She has this wonderful glow about her to where it blinds me

If I had a chance to love her, this would be my pledge to thee

If she was mine, I would give my life to protect hers

If I was rich, to make her mine, I would give up the cars, the money, the diamonds, and the furs.

My life would be fulfilled by hers and hers by mine.

I wish I can tell her out of all the females, I think she is so fine.

Life's Atonement

I wonder what life would be if I were not born

If life would be so much better if I was gone.

I wonder if I'd be missed or if anyone would truly care,

Because in this life I feel the despair.

Sometimes I feel that I cannot take another moment alone,

Due to my past sins, I try to atone

For all the wrong I have done to those who are close to me.

I am thinking to myself, what is God trying to get me to see.

There is something out there that makes me explore,

All I am doing is scraping the surface trying to get to the core,

Of what makes me who I am and who I want to be,

So here I am trying to get through to God, to achieve that point of connectivity.

I sometimes do not understand why I am happy for one minute and the other I am down,

I will smile for a second and the next I will frown.

I wonder why I sleep so much to only realize the joy I get out of lying in a coma,

Feeling so down but what sometimes wakes me is the sweet aroma

Of a French vanilla candle or someone calling my name

So when I wake up everything still feels the same.

I find myself drifting back into my dream world,

Feeling like that oyster that has lost the pearl.

I can't seem to break free from this everyday routine,

Trying to get rid of the dirt of this soul and start clean.

There is no one out there who can truly understand what my life is like so I spend my time by myself because that is all I know.

It would take a special person to help me to grow.

Until that time comes but I do not wait for her at all or even to see if she calls,

Because I have been waiting 36 winters, springs, summers, and falls

And I am still alone for another winter but sleep seems to be my best friend,

It keeps me sane and from me going off the deep end.

I know that sleep is not a good way to spend the day,

So either I will listen to my iPod or read a Shakespearean play.

I love writing poetry because it eases the mind and releases stress,

If God did not give me this talent, I would be a complete mess.

I thank God for the gift to use words in a way that will benefit me and those whom I befriend,

I want to express myself in a way that I know that I will see God's face and peace in the end.

If I Had My Way

When I first saw you, I could not but wonder.

A lot of thoughts go through my head and I start to ponder,

Of what it would be like to have you in my world.

The smile it would bring to my face if you were my girl.

I know you have a man but I wish you were single.

For you and I to get to know each other and for us to mingle.

When I look at you, you are beautiful to me.

Why is it that with me is where I want you to be?

If You Only Knew

If you only knew

How much I care for you

If you only knew

My love will always be true

If you only knew

I will be by your side will never leave

If you only knew

My love is here so please open up
your heart and receive

If you only knew

What I would go through to win
your heart

If you only knew

That I don't want to see us apart

If you only knew

That I would want us to build a
foundation

    If you only knew

That we can overcome any temptation

    If you only knew

What I felt when I get lonely

    If you only knew

That I would love to be your one and only

    If you only knew

How much you mean to me

    If you only knew

That we can make history

    If you only knew

That love is not blind, so I need you to see

    If you only knew

That if you let me, I will love you for all eternity.

In My Life

I have been through so much in my life. I have dealt with relationships and realize that meeting the right female is like finding a needle in a haystack. Is finding that special someone too much to ask for in life? I just want to meet someone that is down to earth, spontaneous, loving, who enjoys walks in the park and on the beach. She has to love kids. I want to be warmed at night by her touch and her smile. I want to be moved by her elegance and her style. I want to be dazzled by her beauty and by her grace. I want to see the sparkle in her eyes and the glow on her face. I want to know that there are butterflies in her stomach whenever I am around. I want to know that I fill her life with joy compared to kids when they are entertained by a clown.

Independence Day

All the events up to this day, have me thinking why did I bother in the first place.

Why couldn't this person say what she had to say to my face.

I am to the point of not putting my feelings out there.

I think about the time spent expressing myself as I stare,

And watch the sunset as it displays this beautiful glare.

She made me well aware how life is not fair.

She messed it up for any other woman who comes into my life.

I am not looking for anything with any female and no longer searching for a wife.

I know they say when you look, you will never find.

This time is my life, I wish I can press rewind.

Love in the mind of one without faith, can be an imaginary tale that will never come true.

I cannot say that this will be the last time that I will say to a woman "I Love You."

I tried to show that I cared for this woman and it was meant for her to stay.

From this day forward, September 7, 2005, will be my Independence Day.

Love is Pain

There is a topic that leaves me with a bad taste, love.

I've noticed that love is just a big waste.

That the love between two people can never exist.

It's like a dream never coming true or time wasted on a wish.

Love is a fable and can never be stable.

Love carries along a barrier that the two cannot cross.

Being in love is meaningless and it leaves both individuals lost.

Rainbow in the Sky

Fairy tales can come true,
It can happen for you.

I want to be your prince charming.

I want to be the rainbow in your sky
that comes out of the blue.

We all know that the rainbow comes
after the storm.

After the clouds disappear that the
rainbow starts to form.

There is a difference between the
rainbow and myself, the rainbow
will soon disappear.

Through all the storms of your life, I
will always be there.

But not me alone because God is
there with us.

It's in Him that we should place our
trust.

As long as He gives me strength, I'll
always have your back no matter if

you're right or wrong and I know you'll do the same for me.

I know we are going to have our differences and on some things we'll agree.

You're probably asking what I will have in store next.

Part two is coming like a sequel to a movie after you read this text.

A Rainbow in the Sky (Part Two)

I never want you to question how I feel or ask why.

A rainbow has different colors with the background of sky blue.

I feel like I have a new life and everything is brand new.

I've been thinking about the future of what I want and who I want to share it with.

I know tomorrow is not promised but if we get there, I want us to share God's gift.

I want you to be happy and give you a life where you will be secure.

I want to provide for you and to give you all you need and more.

I am not just talking about material things but mental as well.

I would be proud when people ask who is your man, you would say, his name is Marcel.

God has been good to me and I am ashamed to call on His name.

You are very special to me and I pray that you feel the same.

So Many Reasons

There are so many reasons why I
feel the way I do.

There are many more of why I am in
love with you.

There are twelve reasons for my
feelings which show my tender side.

I want you to know that you telling
your secrets, in me, you can confide.

I do not want to give you any reason
why you cannot trust me.

For what you know about me, I have
always shown respect and honesty.

My reason for loving you is plain
and simple and I think you know.

So if you don't, I am willing to go all
out and I want to show,

That I can be the man of your
dreams that centers on reality.

I would never overstep my bounds
or invade your privacy.

I know you need your space and that is what I am willing to give.

I promise I will always love you as long as I live.

Everything I say is true and I know that it is hard for you to believe.

Please open up your arms because I have a love that I want you to receive.

There isn't any pressure or a rush with what I want for you.

Times we share leave me with a smile on my face.

The feeling that you give me, I know that no one can replace.

Every time I am with you, I know that everything will be OK.

The day you speak those three words to me is what I can't wait for.

To think about it, I could wait because I want you to mean it with your heart.

The bond we share is all the reason for us to never be apart.

The Existence of a Matchless Beauty

Time heals the heart in the life that God has given.

I just want to know that there is someone for me to grow old with in this life that I am living.

I still question her existence but I still have hope.

I believe that God has someone out there for us all.

Someone we can depend on with just one phone call.

My mind tells me not to give up and still try,

To search for that someone special who can make me smile when I am feeling down.

I am so happy when I know she is around.

I want to experience the special times with her and watch her laugh.

I want to experience what she is like on her good days and when she is on a warpath.

I want to know the good and the bad that is in her style.

I want to know what her lips feel like as we kiss for a while.

I want to feel that there cannot be another that can compare,

That nothing can add up to the times that she and I share

This One Thing I Do Know

I will not know of the what, where how, why or when.

This one thing I do know is that I love you and I have to say it through this pen.

I definitely will not know what tomorrow may hold.

This one thing I do know is that you will keep me safe when the world treats me cold.

I definitely will not know if the sun may rise on the next day.

This one thing I do know is that in my heart is where I want you to stay.

I will not know what the weather may be on tomorrow.

This one thing I do know is that I will not cause you any pain or sorrow.

This is written for the woman who brought happiness in my life.

Those Eight Weeks

From the first week that we met, the little conversations here and there were great.

The second week, it started to progress into me believing in fate.

The third week, consisted of the late conversations and walking you to your train.

The fourth week, I never knew we would spend this time together and letting you go would give me so much pain.

The fifth week, we started opening up to each other about what we have been through.

The sixth week, we would share a kiss and a little more, I did not have a clue.

The seventh week brought about the pure treasures of loving someone truly.

The eighth week brought the demise
and rust of those treasures and I
never knew that the last man
standing was not me.

What Must I Do

What must I do to meet a woman just like you? Do I have to be disrespectful like some brothers, to get your attention? It seems to me that I should not have to act like the others. I want to stand out but that seems too hard when you try to be the nice guy. So I continue to ignore the situation rather than have a confrontation with the opposite sex.

This leaves me wondering and saying what I must do to create that wall that separates me from these women so they would just leave me alone. I try to leave my past and make a way to atone for me walking away and not giving some females a chance. I say this not for me, I close my eyes and upon opening them at a glance what do I see but two more females sitting right in front of me. I do my best to try to ignore them and not look their way but one of them catches my eye but I have no clue, so if any female can help, "What Must I Do"?

What Would It Take

What would it take for a brother like me to get to know you?

No disrespect, if it came down to us being together, I would be true.

I am not here to fill your head with lies but I want to give you the truth and no pain.

If you have time I'll tell you a little about myself, I'll explain.

I am a down to earth brother who would have your best interest at heart.

I would always want to see you happy and never want us to be apart.

I would want to always be in your life especially when you need to talk.

It doesn't matter how busy I am, I would meet you in Central Park so we can walk or take that carriage ride down Fifth Avenue.

I know that we are going to have our arguments but never want to go weeks mad at you or you being mad at me because I really care.

As our time together grows, there are a lot of things that I want us to share.

If we come to the conclusion that we make this exclusive, no one else can compare.

So no matter what may happen in our life together, good or bad, I will always be fair.

I will always be honest with you and I hope I get the same in return.

I am willing to take this slow because if I go too fast, I will crash and burn.

This poem gets to the heart of what I want and what I am willing to offer.

If I get you to be in my life, I will have you picked up by my chauffeur.

I would never sell you short of anything you deserve.

If I treat you in a way that is not right, well I have some nerve.

I will end this by saying that I will always love thee.

When a Man Loves a Woman

There is a love that is not stronger than the love of God.

But it is pleasing in His sight and in no way or shape odd.

This love has a greater power and with the right two people it cannot be broken.

The little things that they do for each other is just a small token,

Of what love can be and what it can become,

So where does all this stem from.

There is a root that extends deep from a man's soul,

To win the heart of the woman he loves, he is paying the toll.

Working night and day to prove his love.

Both of them know their blessings come from above.

Here is the love that blows the mind and that through the test of time it will stand.

The love for this woman is given willingly by this man.

When Will My Time Come

I wait for the day when my time will come.

It gets harder to focus on adding to get the sum.

It starts off good but down the road, I find myself alone.

Love is pain and for all the ups and downs, I try to atone.

For all the heartache I've caused but cannot change the past.

I want to feel loved and someone to hold at last.

I wait patiently for that someone special to enter my world.

I am looking for that diamond to cut me out of this glass and not just a pearl.

I keep saying to myself my day will come soon.

Every year, I wait from January to June,

I also wait July to December,

To share those special times that we both will always remember.

I keep in mind that she will find me when the time is right.

Sometimes I feel she has come and gone and she is no longer in my sight.

It feels like my heart is in this black hole that there is no escape from.

Every day I ask myself this one question, "When Will My Time Come"?

www.ingramcontent.com/pod-product-compliance
Lightning Source LLC
Chambersburg PA
CBHW051712090426
42736CB00013B/2668